AT HOME

A VISIT IN FOUR LANGUAGES

by Esther Hautzig   illustrated by Aliki

THE MACMILLAN COMPANY · NEW YORK

COLLIER-MACMILLAN LIMITED · LONDON

French, Spanish and Russian words and phonetics by the editorial staff of Berlitz Publications, Inc.

For Dorothy and Ben
who made me
at home

Home is the best place in all the world.

It is wonderful to be together with your family in familiar comfortable rooms ...

in Chicago

lamp
lampe
lahmp

lámpara
lahm-pah-rah

лампа
lahm-pah

clock
pendule
pahn-dewl

reloj
reh-lohkh

часы
chah-see

books
livres
leevr

libros
lee-brohs

КНИГИ
k'nee-ghee

dresser
commode
koh-mohd

tocador
toh-kah-dohr

комод
kah-mohd

bed
lit
lee

cama
kah-mah

кровать
krah-vaht'

or Marseilles

sink
évier
eh-v'yeh

fregadero
freh-gah-deh-roh

кухонная раковина
koo-khon-nah-yah rah-kah-vee-nah

cupboard
buffet
bew-feh

aparador
ah-pah-rah-dohr

шкаф для посуды
shkahf dl'yah pah-soo-dee

glasses
verres
vehr

vasos
vah-sohs

стаканы
stah-kah-nee

plates
assiettes
ah-s'yeht

platos
plah-tohs

тарелки
tah-r'yehl-kee

Barcelona

window
fenêtre
fuh-nehtr
ventana
vehn-tah-nah
окно
ahk-noh

table
table
tahbl
mesa
meh-sah
стол
stohl

spoons
cuillères
kwee-yehr
cucharas
koo-chah-rahs
ложки
loh-shkee

stove
cuisinière
kwee-zee-n'yehr
cocina
koh-thee-nah
плита
plee-tah

bowl
bol
bohl
tazón
tah-thohn
миска
mees-kah

sofa
divan
dee-vahn
sofá
soh-fah
диван
dee-vahn

curtains
rideaux
ree-doh
cortinas
kohr-tee-nahs
занавески
zah-nah-v'yeh-skee

pillows
oreillers
oh-reh-yeh
almohadones
ahl-moh-ah-doh-nehs
подушки
pah-doosh-kee

chair
chaise
shehz
silla
seel-yah
стул
stool

To be at home is
always fun, but it is
especially exciting
when family and friends
come to visit.

There is so much to do
before the party begins ...

in Chicago

cook
cuisiner
kwee-zee-neh
cocinar
koh-thee-nahr
варить
vah-reet'

bake
cuire
kweer
hornear
ohr-neh-ahr
печь
p'yehch

decorate
décorer
deh-koh-reh
decorar
deh-koh-rahr
украшать
oo-krah-shaht'

or Marseilles

sweep
balayer
bah-leh-yeh
barrer
bah-rrehr
подметать
pahd-m'yeh-taht

set the table
mettre la table
mehtr lah tahbl
poner la mesa
poh-nehr lah meh-sah
накрывать на стол
nah-kree-vaht' nah stohl

Barcelona

brush the teeth

se brosser les dents
suh broh-seh leh dahng

cepillarse los dientes
theh-pee-l'yahr-seh lohs d'yehn-tehs

чистить зубы
chee-steet' zoo-bee

wash

se laver
suh lah-veh

lavarse
lah-vahr-seh

умываться
oo-mee-vah-tsah

or Leningrad

comb
peigner
peh-n'yeh
peinar
pay-nahr
причёсывать
pree-ch'yoh-see-vhat'

dress
s'habiller
sah-b'yeh
vestirse
vehs-teer-seh
одеваться
ah-d'yeh-vah-tsah

The guests arrive!

Mother serves many
delicious foods
at the party…

in Chicago

butter
beurre
buhr
mantequilla
mahn-teh-kee-l'yah
масло
mah-slah

soup
soupe
soop
sopa
soh-pah
суп
soop

milk
lait
leh
leche
leh-cheh
молоко
mah-lah-koh

salt
sel
sehl
sal
sahl
соль
sohl

pepper
poivre
pwahvr
pimienta
pee-m'yehn-tah
перец
p'yeh-r'yehts

peas
petits pois
p'tee pwah
guisantes
ghee-sahn-tehs
зелёный горошек
z'yeh-l'yoh-nee gah-roh-sheck

potatoes
pommes de terre
pohm duh tehr
patatas
pah-tah-tahs
картофель
car-toh-f'yehl'

fish
poisson
pwah-sohng
pescado
pehs-kah-doh
рыба
ree-bah

bread
pain
pehng
pan
pahn
хлеб
khl'yehp

Barcelona

water
eau
oh

agua
ah-gwah

вода
vah-dah

olives
olives
oh-leev

olivas
oh-lee-vahs

маслины
mah-slee-nee

chicken and rice
poulet au riz
poo-leh oh ree

arroz con pollo
ah-rroth kohn poh-l'yoh

цыплёнок с рисом
tsee-plyoh-nahk s'ree-sahm

fruit
fruit
frwee
fruta
froo-tah
фрукты
frook-tee

tea
thé
teh
té
teh
чай
chigh

sugar
sucre
sewkr
azúcar
ah-thoo-kahr
сахар
sah-khahr

pastry
pâtisserie
pah-tee-sree
pasteles
pahs-teh-lehs
печенье
p'yeh-ch'yeh-n'y

Everyone sings and
laughs and tells
funny stories as they
sit around the table
and enjoy one
another's company...

in Chicago

father
papa
pah-pah
papá
pah-pah
папа
pah-pah

sister
soeur
suhr
hermana
ehr-mah-nah
сестра
s'yeh-strah

aunt
tante
tahnt
tía
tee-ah
тётя
t'yoh-t'yah

or Marseilles

uncle
oncle
ohnkl

tío
tee-oh

дядя
d'yah-d'yah

mother
maman
mah-mahng

mamá
mah-mah

мама
mah-mah

grandfather
grand-père
grahn-pehr

abuelo
ah-bweh-loh

дедушка
d'yeh-doosh-kah

grandmother
grand'mère
grahn-mehr

abuela
ah-bweh-lah

бабушка
bah-boo-shkah

Barcelona

great-grandmother
arrière grand'mère
ah-r'yehr grahn-mehr
bisabuela
bee-sah-bweh-lah
прабабушка
prah-bah-boosh-kah

cousins
cousins
koo-zehng
primos
pree-mohs
двоюродные
dvah-you-rahd-nee-yeh

brother
frère
frehr
hermano
ehr-mah-noh
брат
braht

or Leningrad

friend
amie
ah-mee
amiga
ah-mee-gah
приятельница
pree-yah-t'yehl-nee-tsah

neighbors
voisins
vwah-zehng
vecinos
veh-thee-nohs
соседи
sah-s'yeh-dee

On quiet days
when it rains or snows
and you cannot go
outside there is
always something
to do...

in Chicago

paint
peindre
pehndr
pintar
peehn-tahr
рисовать красками
ree-sah-vaht krah-skah-mee

build
construire
kohns-trweer
construir
kohns-troo-eer
строить
stroh-eat'

paste
coller
koh-leh
pegar
peh-gahr
клеить
klyeh-eat'

listen

écouter
eh-koo-teh

escuchar
ehs-koo-chahr

слушать
sloo-shaht

play

jouer
zhoo-eh

jugar
hoo-gahr

играть
ee-graht'

Barcelona

read
lire
leer

leer
leh-ehr

читать
chee-taht'

embroider
broder
broh-deh

bordar
bohr-dahr

вышивать
vee-shee-vaht'

or Leningrad

explore
explorer
ehks-ploh-<u>reh</u>
explorar
ehks-ploh-<u>rahr</u>
исследовать
ees-sl'yeh-dah-vaht'

But no matter where you go, to distant places or just around the corner, it always feels good to come back home to Chicago or **Marseilles,** **Barcelona** or **Leningrad.**

Additional Words

English	French	Spanish	Russian
home	maison *meh-zohng*	casa *kah-sah*	дома *doh-mah*
family	famille *fah-mee*	familia *fah-mee-l'yah*	семья *s'yeh-m'yah*
rooms	pièces *p'yehs*	cuartos *kwahr-tohs*	комнаты *koh-mnah-tee*
bedroom	chambre à coucher *shahmbr ah koo-sheh*	dormitorio *dohr-mee-toh-r'yoh*	спальня *spah-l'n'yah*
kitchen	cuisine *kwee-zeen*	cocina *koh-thee-nah*	кухня *koo'kh-n'yah*
living room	salle de séjour *sahl duh seh-zhoor*	sala *sah-lah*	гостиная *gah-stee-nah'yah*
party	réception *reh-sehp-s'yohng*	fiesta *f'yehs-tah*	вечеринка *v'yeh-ch'yeh-reen-kah*
visit	visite *vee-zeet*	visita *vee-see-tah*	посещение *pah-s'yeh-shch'yeh-nee-yeh*
guests	invités *ehng-vee-teh*	invitados *een-vee-tah-dohs*	гости *goh-stee*
Chicago	Chicago *shee-kah-go*	Chicago *chee-kah-goh*	Чикаго *chee-kah-gah*
Marseilles	Marseille *mahr-seh*	Marsella *mahr-seh-l'yah*	Марсель *mahr-s'yehl'*
Barcelona	Barcelone *bahr-suh-lon*	Barcelona *bahr-theh-loh-nah*	Барселона *bahr-s'yeh-loh-nah*
Leningrad	Leningrad *leh-neen-grahd*	Leningrado *leh-neehn-grah-doh*	Ленинград *l'yeh-neen-grahd*

Russian Alphabet

А	а	ah as in <u>a</u>rch	П	п	p as in <u>p</u>ie
Б	б	b as in <u>b</u>oy	Р	р	r as in po<u>rr</u>idge
В	в	v as in <u>v</u>oice	С	с	s as in <u>s</u>tay
Г	г	g as in <u>g</u>ood	Т	т	t as in <u>t</u>oy
Д	д	d as in <u>d</u>o	У	у	oo as in f<u>oo</u>t
Е	е	yeh as in <u>ye</u>t	Ф	ф	f as in <u>f</u>ix
Ё	ё	yoh as in <u>yo</u>yo	Х	х	kh as in <u>h</u>ot
Ж	ж	zh as in plea<u>s</u>ure	Ц	ц	ts as in le<u>t's</u> go
З	з	z as in <u>z</u>ero	Ч	ч	ch as in <u>ch</u>urch
И	и	ee as in f<u>ee</u>t	Ш	ш	sh as in <u>sh</u>ort
Й	й	y as in <u>y</u>east	Щ	щ	shch as in bor<u>shch</u>
К	к	k as in <u>k</u>eep	Ъ	ъ	separation sign (')
Л	л	l as in <u>l</u>uck	Ы	ы	ih as in a drawn-out <u>is</u>
М	м	m as in <u>m</u>e	Ь	ь	soft sign (preceding consonant pronounced as if <u>ee</u> followed)
Н	н	n as in <u>n</u>ow			
О	о	oh as in <u>o</u>ften when stressed, closer to ah when unstressed	Э	э	eh as in <u>e</u>mpty
			Ю	ю	yuh as <u>you</u>
			Я	я	yah as in <u>ya</u>rd

the end

fin

fin

КОНЕ́Ц